Photographic Memory for Beginners

A Practical Guide to Limitless Memory

Dane Krauss

CONTENTS

INTRODUCTION

Memories are crucial to us as human beings because, in so many ways, it helps shape who we are. They work as an internal biography of our lives, documenting the things that happened to us, what we've done, and make the stories we tell about ourselves. Memory serves as the sum total of what we remember and helps us learn from previous experiences. Consider for a moment how many times in a day you rely on your memory to help you with passwords, finding directions, or greeting someone on their birthday. Human memory makes all these things possible and more. The retrieval of relevant information is something we all do on a regular, daily basis, and whether we realise it or not, we rely so much on memories more than we ever accomplish. Some memories are brief, while others can be stored for a long time, and possibly throughout our whole lifetime. In order to make new memories, our brain processes information and stores them for later use. And while this is usually done far from our awareness, this formed memory is kept ready for retrieval when the time comes for us to need them.

Owing to the fact that memories are so important to us, its loss can be very frustrating and can have devastating effects on our daily lives. And while age-related memory loss is inevitable, there are many different ways to preserve the integrity of this process through memory enhancement exercises. This book will explore the many methods and techniques that can help you improve your memory, enhance brain function, and will help you develop proven ways to preserve your memory.

CHAPTER 1 – MEMORY PALACE

You might know who Sherlock Holmes is, and for a good reason. Not only is he the most famous fictional detective there ever was, but his amazing feats of being able to solve countless mysteries and puzzles are all thanks to his powerful use of memory retrieval techniques. He makes use of what is known as the memory palace technique.

The memory palace is one of the most powerful memory techniques available, but what makes it even more interesting is that it's been around since ancient Rome. According to the popular myth, this technique was developed by Simonides, a Greek poet. He was attending a banquet when two men called him outside. When he arrived outside, the building behind him collapsed, crushing everyone who attended the party. However, Simonides was able to identify all the crushed bodies inside, supposedly because he remembered where and who sat at every location in the banquet hall. This technique of being able to remember based on location came to be known as the memory palace or mind palace.

In order to do this, one must first visualise a place or location he or she is familiar with. This can be the layout of a house or the directions to the daily commute to work. This place will be used to store the set of memories used for physically remembering memories. The steps are outlined as follows:

1.   Choose a place

The effectiveness of this technique is based on how familiar you are with your chosen place. So make sure this is something that you know very well, without making too much effort to make out the details of the particular place.

The next is to ensure that you build a specific walk-through in that place instead of picturing it as a still-life scene. For example, you may visualise the neighbourhood in your work area, so you can try to picture out the usual route you take when going to your workplace. If using your own house, mentally walk through the door where you usually enter, all the way through the exit. This will help you keep track of items you will be recalling in order later on.

2. List the distinctive features

As you start your mental walk-through, take note of the things and distinctive features you encounter. For example, you might notice your bright blue front door when you enter the house. As you go inside, you are standing right next to a yellow coat hanger. Then moving along, you pass by the TV room with the big potted plant near the doorway. As you move along, continue to note these features and make them stand out. These are the details that will be of utmost importance to you later on.

3. Have the place imprinted on your mind

This step is crucial because the ability to remember and make a memory of the things you want to recall relies on how well you know your memory palace. This is why it is recommended that you choose a place or a house that you know very well. To make sure that you are 100% familiar with it, the following methods can be performed:

• Do a physical walk-through inside the house, noting the distinctive features you want to employ later on. Repeat these things out loud for retention.

• Write down these distinctive features and repeat them out loud while mentally walking through them.

• Ensure that every time you do this mental walk-through, you are seeing these distinctive features from the same vantage point.

What you need to realise is that you can never get too familiar with this memory palace of yours. In fact, it is better that you "overlearn" this so that it becomes muscle memory the more you practice recalling this.

4. Designate and associate

Now that you have your visual associations in place, you can take each distinctive feature and associate it with the element you want to memorise. In fact, there is a right way to do this. To ensure that retention happens, make the association as crazy and as absurd as possible. Make it offensive, animated, unusual, and nonsensical – all the things that are sure to pop and stand out in your head. Make it so unique that the possibility of it happening in real life is zero.

Let's go back to that bright blue door. Now, imagine you are using your memory palace to remember your grocery list. You may picture out the bright blue door with a frame of a single egg hanging. This is, in fact, Humpty Dumpty and he's about to fall off the hanging frame. Next, you go to your yellow coat stand. There is an army of broccolis – little green veggies that are trying to climb up the stand. As you can see, your grocery list is hidden among the few details peppered throughout the house, coupled with an absurd animation and story. Do the same for the rest of the memory palace and make the story as crazy as you can.

5.   Retrieval and recall

Now that you've built your memory palace, you can revisit this place anytime you want in order to recall the associated items. You will soon discover that with practice in visualising, you will be able to effortlessly retrieve the memorised items instantly as you look at the journey's selected features. Walk through the memory palace a couple more times, and when you find yourself at the end of the journey, imagine turning back around in the opposite direction and back to the start.

As humans, we tend to be generally bad at remembering things. But the memory palace is all about changing your memories into images that are more familiar and to place them in a mental location that you know very well. Since information and data tend to be just floating around in our brains, our goal is to give these things a structure for them to anchor on. When that happens, we provide context and order to the things we want to remember.

While the use of the memory palace is still relatively unknown, it can be very helpful in aiding you to memorise large bits of information. This technique can be used by a student trying to pass an exam, or a traveller who wants to be fluent in Spanish, or even to an ordinary person who just wants to stick to the grocery list on a run to the mall. Whatever the desired outcome is, the memory palace is a great way to help you achieve your goals.

Perhaps one of the most important benefits one gets from the memory palace technique is its use for our ageing minds. We're all ageing as we speak and even as you are reading this book. With age comes deterioration, and our memories get weaker. There are certain situations that can leave us feeling frustrated due to these changes. But studies have shown that the use of memory palace holds promise in aiding the enhancement of the ageing brain. While it doesn't reverse the weakening of the memories, it can be the perfect solution towards occasional forgetfulness. And with constant practice, the brain becomes more elastic.

Mind's Eye

There is a saying that goes, "the eyes look, but the brain sees." Is there really a difference between looking and seeing?

We think of the eyes as cameras, able to capture the images that we see and interact with in the outside world. In reality, our view of the world is a result of the illusion our individual brains process from what our eyes input into it. This input is also constantly shifting, and our brains tend to filter out unnecessary movements as it scans the environment in detail. From this information, the brain translates it into an image that we can understand. In fact, the brain is only able to receive three images for each second, and these are designated and associated with earlier memories or information in order to provide the experience of your current reality. Think of it as a machine that runs constantly at all times. In order to protect the brain from overheating, it needs to save energy by choosing what is worth looking at.

In this regard, we may be familiar with the feeling of looking at something inside our brains, conjuring up images even when these images aren't directly in front of us. This is what we call the mind's eye. It's the mental ability of being able to conceive imaginary or recollected scenes. It is akin to the mental picture we get in our mind. If I tell you to think of a pink elephant on tiptoes, balancing on a ball, you would be able to conjure this image just as easily as if you've seen it in real life. In brain scans, neural patterns light up when you are given the task to imagine something with your mind's eye. This indicates that there is a part of your brain that actively seeks to come up with the image or recollected images.

As a memory enhancing technique, mind's eye refers to a method known as sensory discrimination. It requires you to ignore distractions when we are actively focused on something we are paying attention to. In the Mind's eye exercise, you can be asked to remember a target image and point out whether a set of images contain that specific target image. It targets visual memory and retention as the images become more similar, changes patterns, or if you are tasked to remember more than one image at a time.

The use of the mind's eye is undoubtedly an important aspect of building your memory palace. How else will you be able to visualise the house you will be placing your associations on? And if you put animations on your associations, you will need to create vivid images in order to make them memorable. This form of visualisation needs to be sharpened up in order to enhance recall skills and mental imagery. Think of memories as encoded like a jigsaw puzzle, with associations linked together. The stronger and more vivid these associations are, the more effective one can access a memory.

Let's take a look at how the famous detective, Sherlock Holmes, does this technique. In "A Scandal in Bohemia," there is an exchange between Holmes and his partner, Watson, that goes like this:

"Quite so," he answered, lighting a cigarette, and throwing himself down into an armchair. "You see, but you do not observe. The distinction is clear. For example, you have frequently seen the steps that lead up from the hall to this room."

"Frequently."

"How often?"

"Well, some hundreds of times."

"Then how many are there?"

"How many? I don't know."

"Quite so! You have not observed. And yet you have seen. That is just my point. Now, I know that there are seventeen steps because I have both seen and observed."

This exchange shows us that Holmes has developed keen observational skills regardless of any environment he was in. He was never observing, and never out of touch with his surroundings. This kind of mindfulness is almost superhuman, yet with constant practice, this feat can be performed by anyone just as easily.

We often block our sense to the world, using only one or two sensations, when, in fact, we can experience situations through multi-sensory perceptions. This means we should limit ourselves to our senses – use your sense of hearing, touch, taste, or smell when appropriate. While Holmes' keen observation astounds us, it is certainly not a superhuman ability. He wasn't born with it, but he spent a lifetime cultivating habits of mindfulness. He chose to observe, at all times, regardless of circumstances.

Our worst habit is not paying enough attention. This is even more pronounced in this day and age, wherein we would always choose to distract and block ourselves from the outside world by putting on headphones, or wearing dark sunglasses. We choose to limit the use of our senses, thereby allowing us to not fully enjoy and bask in the details of our surroundings. But despite these bad habits, the great thing about our brains is that we can always rewire the way it works, in a way that mindfulness eventually becomes less of an effort.

If you find yourself struggling to pay attention, you can do any of the following:

• Work into it every day. Putting in the effort will pay off, and because you need observational skills to become a habit, you will need to do it every single day. You can try to take in one interesting picture a day, or take note of your co-worker's tie daily. Whatever it is, choose to become more observant about one specific thing until it starts to become effortless.

• Write it down. One of the best and effective ways to help you remember and become observant is to write or draw the things you observe. It can be done at any time of the day, regardless of what you are doing. For example, dedicate 5 minutes during your break time at work and write down the things you observe from your colleague's behaviour. Pay attention to how they talk, how they animate when talking, their gestures, or how they take a sip of water. The more you do this on paper, the better you get at observing.

• Start making connections. Just like using the memory palace, associations are important. After all, the increased focus and critical thinking aren't going to help you much when you can't make connections between the knowledge you have and what you see.

• Expand your knowledge base. Remain curious about a lot of different things. This will help you increase your associations and make them even more interesting and relatable to you.

The memory palace and mind's eye are concepts that not only improve memory, but can also be used as coping strategies for people who have difficulty with visualisation. In the case of children with Attention-deficit Hyperactivity Disorder, having a weak working memory is something that is all too common. One way to go about this is assigning objects that rhyme with numbers. Let's say, 1-sun, two-shoe, 3-tree, and so on. In order to learn new information, the child can simply visualise this number rhyme interacting with the things to memorise. If he is tasked to bring a book, an eraser, and a notebook, he might do it this way: a book about suns and planets, a shoe with an eraser on the bottom so it doesn't ever leave shoeprints, and a notebook caught high up in a tree. You will soon find out that the ADHD brain loves variety and novelty. Working with your child to improve their weak working memory may take time, but it will be worth it.

Being mindful creates greater awareness between the environment and ourselves. The realm of observing goes beyond just seeing – but involves a closer look at details in order to enhance our memory keeping.

CHAPTER 2 – METHOD OF LOCI

"I consider that a man's brain originally is like a little empty attic, and you have to stock it with such furniture as you choose."
- Sherlock Holmes

The earliest known mnemonic strategy is called "method of loci," with loci meaning place or location. Its premise lies on our familiarity with certain places and attaching something you need to remember these places. In effect, the places will serve as your clues to recollection. This concept may already seem familiar to you by now, especially after the first chapter of this book, but in essence, the method of loci is the basic underlying principle for memory palace. Method of loci is all about remembering something based on a familiar location and its association to an object, while the memory palace or mind palace deals with a pre-learned set of locations that make up a whole "house" or "palace." In short, memory palace is a sequence of locations that one can find useful for the method of loci.

Apart from using the mind's eye, the method of loci can also be learned through other senses. Those who are deficient in one sense tend to overcompensate and excel in their remaining senses. But these senses can be trained and developed regardless of whether you have or don't have the loss of a particular sense. Examples are learning Braille for tactile sense, wine aroma kits for olfactory sense, and perfect pitch exercises for the auditory sense.

Wine educators and their students use aroma kits to increase their knowledge about the specific ingredients found in wine. With constant practice, one can learn to develop a personal scent memory to eventually distinguish the nuances in wines or whisky.

Perfect pitch is the rare ability to be able to identify, sing, or play back the exact same note. If you were to play a C# on the piano, the one with perfect pitch would be able to tell you that you've just played a C#. And if that piano was out of tune, he'd be the first to know. While most studies show that having perfect pitch is genetic, it is a skill that can be learned early in life. However, as we age, our brains lose some of its neuroplasticity, and it becomes harder for us to train and develop skills like this. Studies claimed that people with perfect pitch can subconsciously allocate musical notes to their memory and will be able to process them later. This gives them the ability to accurately identify notes without any outside reference.

Blind people are known to have far superior perceptual abilities in their remaining senses. One of these is their tactile sense, as evidenced by the mastery of the Braille reading system. However, sighted people can also be trained in simple sensory tasks that can eventually progress later on.

Transferring Memory Palaces

Now that you've settled on your memory palace, you may begin to wonder: can I transfer from one place to another? If not, can I override, delete, or re-use the same memory palace over and over again?

The quick answer to all these is: yes, you can do all these things. Since our individuality allows us to choose what works best for us, there is simply no limit as to how many times you can recycle the same memory palace over and over again, or to retain more than 10 memory palaces at a time. However, take note that this can be most effective when using long-term memories, and not for high-speed working memories, such as those used in rapid-fire competitive play.

Before you create another memory palace, make sure you are 100% familiar with your current one. The same principle applies when you choose to override the old data in order to make space for new ones. Another technique is to link new data with the old ones, making relevant associations. For example, your first memory palace lists down the presidents of the USA. Then you decide to fill it with a new list of human-crewed spaceships in order. You can associate, say, George Washington riding the Vostok 1, representing the first president of the USA and the first human-crewed spaceship. Do this for the rest of the list until it is fully committed to your memory.

In the case of transferring from one mind palace to another, try to limit the different palaces to less than 6 at a time until you allow yourself to really immerse those details so deep that it becomes ingrained in you. You can then jump from one palace to another, trying out the many different ways and lists you can train to recall.

CHAPTER 3 – MNEMONICS

Mnemonics is a type of memory tool that helps us learn large pieces of information that takes the form of music, acronym, expression or word, model, ode or rhyme, or connection. The concept behind it is to encode hard-to-remember information and hide it in a way that is much easier to recall afterwards.

When assigning mnemonics, there are three fundamental principles you need to know. These are imagination, association, and location.

Imagination is what you need to create strong and vivid images that are potent enough for you to recall later on. The more potent your imagination and visualisation is, the more it will stick with you. This is why it is recommended that you go crazy in making up these mental images. Make it as wild, absurd, violent, or as sensual as you want.

In association, you create linkages between the images and the way you want to remember them.

The use of location is particularly important because it gives you a specific context in which you can recall your information.

Forms of mnemonics

Music

Have you ever wondered why it's easy to remember the lyric to a song, particularly a song that you really like? The same method of being able to memorise the lyrics of a song can be used to remember things in academics or in daily life. In the same way, advertisers make use of jingles about their products in order for customers to remember them. Tunes are very easy to remember, and if you place the information through a song, you may be able to recall more than you expected. An example of this is how we memorise letters by singing the Alphabet Song.

Acronyms

Taking the first letter of every item you want to remember and arranging them in a way that makes more sense and comprehensible to you is called an acronym. One of the most famous acronyms is ROY G BIV, in which each letter represents the first letter of a colour associated with it: red, orange, yellow, green, blue, indigo, and violet.

Expression or word

This is the most popular form of mnemonic use, and it involves making a phrase or sentence out of the first letter of the items. Similar to acronyms, but retention can be stronger because of the coherence of the made-up sentence. For example, the order of operations for math is Parentheses, Exponents, Multiply, Divide, Add, and Subtract. Taking the first letter of each word will give us PEMDAS, which doesn't make sense or is hard to remember. But if we form it into a sentence, such as "Please Excuse My Dear Aunt Sally," the recall can be very strong.

Model

Model mnemonics make use of representations, such as the pyramid model of stages, a circular sequence model, a pie-chart, or a 5-box sequence. This can be seen in samples, such as Maslow's Hierarchy of Needs, wherein each stage in the pyramid represents a specific need, building its way up towards the top, which is self-actualisation.

Ode or rhyme

Find several relevant rhyming words to help you recall. For example, memorising which months of a year have 30, 31, or 28 days respectively can be found in this rhyme:

"30 days has September

April, June, and November

All the rest have 31

Except February alone

For it has 28 days clear

And 29 in each Leap Year"

Connection

This type of mnemonic deals with information to be remembered that is already known, or associating the items to something that sounds like it. When remembering the direction of latitude and longitude, for example, you may picture out long lines across the globe, from North to South that coincides with LONGitude. On the other hand, latitude must run from West to East because there is no N in the word, and it rhymes with the word flat, just as flat line runs horizontally.

CHAPTER 4 – MIND MAPS

To some extent, we are visual learners, and we tend to learn best with visually stimulating aids. One of the best ways to practice this visual memory learning is through the use of mind mapping. Mind maps make use of organisational structures that include the use of lines, symbols, words, images, or colour. It converts an otherwise monotonous list of information into a highly organised diagram in a logical and relatable way. It also helps that information in mind map usually have a natural relationship with all other concepts one is trying to retain. Think of it like a city, wherein the city centre represents the main idea, while the main roads that lead to it are the key concepts in your thought process. The secondary roads represent the secondary thoughts, and so on. Relevant ideas are given symbols or landmarks. You can choose to write down your mind map and study it visually. But with time and practice with this skill, you can effectively whip up a mind map of your own using your mind's eye.

The five essential characteristics of a typical mind map are as follows:

• Main idea represents the subject you are trying to make a mind map on. Put it at the centre. For example, Kinds of Food.

• Main theme branches from the central image. In the above example, we can put Go, Glow, and Grow as separate branches from the central image of Food.

• Branches form a key image from the main theme. You may limit this to a few phrases or words. For example, Go foods give energy, Glow foods give healthy skin, Grow foods make one bigger.

• Associate these branches with images. Examples of Go foods can be riding a bicycle, Glow foods illuminating, and Grow foods sprouting muscles.

• Connected modal structure brings together all these concepts. Feel free to branch out into smaller concepts, making sure everything is connected as a whole.

Again, we go back to the famous detective and how he would do mind mapping. How would Sherlock Holmes do mind mapping? Since he does a lot of mystery solving and detecting murders and thefts, he needs excellent mind mapping skills to be able to solve them. First, he would segregate the evidence into symbols and icons. Then he would attach pictures to the collected pieces of evidence with the help of branches. With the map right-facing him, he would be able to map out and follow the developments of the case, by joining pieces of evidence and information and extending the branches into further information. With the linkages organised clearly, he can make use of keywords and use these to unearth archived cases in order to find relevant and similar themes. From this, he can start ticking off tasks from each list, always finding relationships and linkages that could all lead into one possible scenario.

As you can see, mind mapping techniques of Sherlock Holmes are what we would ordinarily use if we were to make a mind map ourselves. It just takes a bit of practice to do so. You may not be a fictional crime-fighter in the 19th century, but the skills for mind maps can help reveal important connections and patterns in the real world that can be beneficial to you. Apart from enabling you to develop deep knowledge about a specific subject, you can use this technique to do simple tasks and manage them properly.

CHAPTER 5 – PRACTICAL USES FOR MEMORY ENHANCEMENT TECHNIQUES

Wim Hof Method

Try to take a deep breath and exhale. Repeat.

Before you started consciously breathing, you probably weren't thinking about breathing at all. This is because breathing is controlled by our autonomic nervous system, the one that is also responsible for involuntary muscle movements, such as the beating of our hearts, the blinking of our eyes, temperature regulation, and breathing.

The Wim Hof Method (WHM) is known as a series of breathing exercises and cold immersion techniques to manipulate the body into reaping benefits, such as enhanced sleep, improved health, and better memory function. This method was developed by Wim Hof, also known as "The Iceman," as a means to control the body's inner thermostat and regulate temperature. By learning to control the autonomic nervous system, one can have incredible control over his own physiology through the power of his mind. This is made possible by a method that involves deep breathing and holding one's breath for extended periods that eventually results in your ability to progressively hold breaths for a long time.

To do this, you first take a deep breath, breathing in more air than you need to breathe out, and then do a full expiration afterwards. Next, you hold your breath after this exhalation, then take in one big inhalation as a 'recovery breath" that resets you back. This surge of fresh oxygen rushes in through the cells of your body, allowing it to receive the full effect of the exercise. By inducing hypoxia through breath-holding, one creates a positive stress response by turning on the survival mode that allows one to withstand extreme temperatures. It facilitates survival during lower oxygen environments.

A study of this method in rats showed that it helps in the proliferation of neural stem cells, which help in cognitive function and memory. Since stem cells are only able to survive in a state of hypoxia or when oxygen is low, inducing this state can be very beneficial. Another way in which WHM can benefit the brain is that when there is low oxygen tension in the blood, it causes more blood vessels to awaken that may not have been used before, since we only use a limited number of blood vessels every day. By increasing the blood flow to them, the brain can be fully alert, and thus be able to focus and retain more memories. In general, it can help increase focus, energy levels, overall productivity, and keeps a calm mind.

Brain Waves and How to Enhance Them

There are five types of brain waves present in all humans, and each serves an important function to our state of wakefulness, play, or even sleep. Each one helps us cope with various situations, and if either one of them is overproduced or underproduced, it can cause problems. When these brain waves are at their optimum level, it can produce benefits that can improve memory and cognitive functioning. There are various ways to increase them and to enhance each brain frequency. We take a look at each one:

Gamma Waves

These are involved in higher processing tasks, such as learning, memory, and information processing – all higher cognitive functioning around 40Hz gamma waves is thought to be required in order to learn new material. Too much of it can cause anxiety and distress, while having too little can be seen in those with ADHD and learning disabilities. At its optimal level, it can be effective in learning, information processing, cognition, perception, REM sleep, and binding senses. To significantly increase it, meditation works as a method to bring the level back up. It is the brainwave of highest frequency.

Beta Waves

Beta waves are commonly observed when we are awake. With the right amount, it can help us focus in school or at work, allowing conscious thought, logical thinking, and is thought to have a stimulating effect. You may liken it to brain waves that are responsible for people to do critical daily tasks, such as writing, reading, socialisation, and critical thinking. It is also associated with a high level of arousal, in higher beta frequencies. In excess, it can lead to stress, restlessness, and anxiety. Too little of it can lead to frequent daydreaming, depression, or poor cognition. Since it is crucial in our daily tasks, it can help in our problem solving, focus, and memory at its optimum level. To increase it is fairly easy – energy drinks, coffee, and other stimulants can easily do the trick.

Alpha Waves

These waves lie in between our conscious thinking and subconscious mind. When needed, it helps us calm down and relax. Too much can lead to daydreaming, being too relaxed, and the inability to focus. Too little can result in anxiety, inability to sleep, and OCD. To enhance alpha waves, relaxants such as alcohol, marijuana, and depressants can be helpful.

Theta Waves

As long as Theta waves aren't produced in our waking hours, it can be very helpful in our creativity, emotional connection, intuition, and relaxation. Too much theta activity may make people highly suggestible, because of the state of being deeply relaxed and semi-hypnotic. This hyperactivity and inattentiveness is the exact opposite of the effects of low theta waves, which include poor emotional awareness, stress, and anxiety. Depressants help to increase theta waves.

Delta Waves

Delta waves represent the slowest brain waves ever recorded in humans, often found in young children and infants. We tend to produce less of them as we age. Deep levels of relaxation and restorative, healing sleep are associated with delta waves, as with natural healing and immunity. Too much of it is associated with ADHD, inability to think clearly, learning problems, and brain injuries. Having too little can be likened to waking up not feeling refreshed after sleep, and the inability to revitalise or rejuvenate the brain. Depressants and a good night's sleep can help bring it to its optimum level.

How to memorise a pack of cards

Imagine being able to memorise a pack of cards as quickly as they are dealt. Sound impossible? With the right techniques, you can master this and eventually wow your friends and family. All you need is a mental map and a celebrity matrix so effective and familiar to you that you can quickly make up a memory journey right on the spot.

Learning the cards

There are 52 pieces in a deck of cards. The first step is to memorise all of them. But not in a way that you memorise each number and their corresponding symbols. You, instead, convert them into celebrities.

Remember that the mind ignores the mundane but retains the crazy and absurd. To make the association really pop out, assigning celebrities to each suit is the easiest way of recalling a deck of cards. And to make it even easier, make each suit correspond to a personality trait. Hearts can be celebrities you like, diamonds represent the super rich, clubs for tough or crazy people, and spades for amusing or absurd people.

Once the suits are all assigned, it is now time to assign the cards to professions. Make all even number females and all odd numbers males. Make sure they are all paired up. So, for example, you can make 5 powerful men, while 6 all-powerful females, and so on.

Here's a sample of how the assigned cards would look like:

• King and Queen will each represent the male and female parts of a celebrity couple with "royal" status.

• Jack represents religious figures, as they were mostly bachelors. Just like the Jack is.

• The highest numbers, 10 and 9, can represent some of the most powerful men and women.

• 8 and 9 are the men and women who have great physiques.

• Make 6 and 5 represent some of the most controversial male and female celebs.

• Movie stars represent 4 and 3.

• 2 for all women athletes, while Ace is for men athletes.

With these assigned professions, one can then use your existing knowledge to fill up the cards with associated names. A male athlete (ace) who got rich (diamonds) could be Michael Jordan (Ace of Diamonds). Once you have the associations ready, take time to memorise and translate them into images until it becomes automatic.

Create a Memory Palace

You will need to remember 52 spots in your memory palace, and to break this down and make it easier to remember, choose 5 rooms with 10 pieces of furniture each. You can assign your bedroom, bathroom, living room, dining room, and office for this. The 10 pieces of furniture represent things that you might find in that room, and add 2 more pieces of furniture to one room because a deck of cards has 52 pieces.

Going through a deck of cards

Now, the fun begins. Once you have both your memory palace and celebrity matrix memorised fully, you can begin. Just make sure all your associations are 100% ingrained in your brain. Go through a shuffled deck of cards. For every ten cards, assign actions between the associated celebrity to the 10 pieces of furniture of the room. Then move on to the next rooms. For example, your first room is the dining room, and the first furniture is the microwave. Your first card is an Ace of Diamonds, so you can think of Michael Jordan preparing a microwave meal after a game. Assign each character at the position in which they are drawn. Continue to make the associations to the rest of the furniture before moving on to the next room. By segregating the rooms with only 10 pieces of furniture each, you won't get so overwhelmed with the number of objects you need to memorise in one room.

Recalling and retrieving

Now that you have the stories imagined, remember what each suit and number means and go through each room in the order of the furniture you've memorised. By then, you will have been able to enumerate the order of the shuffled deck you've just seen.

Practice makes perfect

The system works, but only with constant practice. Sharpen your mind and try to improve your speed.

Keep it fun

Whether you have plans to use this trick for competition or for amusement, remember to have fun. Retrain, practice, and perform every day until you get better, faster, and the associations become second nature.

Memory for Competitions

Memory athletes wouldn't be where they are today if not for constant and rigorous mental practices over the course of time. Just as physical sports need training, so do mental athletes need exercises. You may eventually want to remember a deck of cards as they are dealt, or memorise a sequence of numbers, or pick out a familiar face in a sea of people. If you plan to develop your memory and expand it to be able to compete, all you really need to do is work daily on the memory techniques presented in this book. Memory champions have used the method of loci and memory palace to enhance associations and linkages. As you progress, you can make these linkages even more compressed, in order to be able to memorise more. For example, let's go back to the deck of card association. Ace of Spades is represented by Michael Jordan. Next time you see this card, imagine Michael Jordan (Ace of Spades) dunking his basketball on the microwave, wearing a jersey with Queen Elizabeth's face (Queen of Hearts), eating the meat dress of Lady Gaga (Six of Spades). As you work on integrating more and more associations, you will become more adept at remembering, bringing you up to speed and improvement.

CONCLUSION

Perhaps Sherlock Holmes was a superhuman detective, with his vast array of mind abilities and powerful memory. But if there's anything that you can take from this book, it's the knowledge that you too can enhance and improve your memory. Whether it's for casual or competition purposes, memory enhancement techniques are very effective at helping you unlock a whole new potential. Apart from impressing your friends and family, the improved focus that comes along with it can continue to stimulate your brain, making it age less faster. Remember that memories are all that we take when all is said and done, and if we let it deteriorate, it can be very devastating. Memory enhancement techniques also serve to keep our brains young and happy, so do your brain a favour and keep it up to its toes in stimulation. You don't need to be Sherlock Holmes, but you can be your own memory champion.

-- Dane Krauss

Dear Reader,

Thanks for exploring this book with me. Now that you know how to develop a photographic memory…

…why not take one step further and learn about the intriguing world of hypnosis?

You'll love the other book on the improvement of the mind, because it complements this one.

Get it now.

Thanks,

Dane

P.S. Reviews are like giving a warm hug to your favourite author. We love hugs.

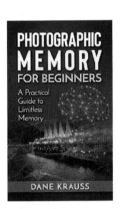

Photographic Memory for Beginners: A Practical Guide to Limitless
Memory
https://www.amazon.com/dp/B07KMBX8RF

Author Biography

Dane Krauss is a budding author who has been fascinated with anything related to the mind…

…ever since he learned to read.

He currently lives in New York … Mind Manipulation for Beginners and Photographic Memory for Beginners are his pride and joy.

When he isn't busy writing, he enjoys a good spot of chess to sharpen his mind.

Check Out Other Books

Mind Manipulation for Beginners: A Practical Guide to Hypnosis
https://www.amazon.com/dp/B07K3CJ562

Made in the USA
Lexington, KY
22 May 2019